THE BLACK COUNTRY
LIVING MUSEUM
25 YEARS

THE BLACK COUNTRY
LIVING MUSEUM
25 YEARS

DAVID F. VODDEN

SUTTON PUBLISHING LIMITED

Sutton Publishing Limited
Phoenix Mill · Thrupp · Stroud
Gloucestershire · GL5 2BU

First published 2000
Reprinted in 2002

Title page photograph: The Rolfe Street
Building, 28 June 2000. This former public
baths building from Smethwick will house
new exhibition halls as well as providing
archive storage and a new entrance hall.
It was finally opened to the public on
8 August 2000. (*D.F. Vodden*)

British Library Cataloguing in Publication Data
A catalogue record for this book is available from the
British Library.

ISBN 0-7509-2629-5

Typeset in 10.5/13.5 Photina.
Typesetting and origination by
Sutton Publishing Limited.
Printed and bound in England
by J.H. Haynes & Co. Ltd, Sparkford.

THE BLACK COUNTRY SOCIETY

This voluntary society, affiliated to the Civic Trust, was founded
in 1967 as a reaction to the trend of the late 1950s and early 1960s
to amalgamate everything into large units and in the Midlands to
sweep away the area's industrial heritage in the process.

The general aim of the Society is to create interest in the past, present and future of
the Black Country, and early on it campaigned for the establishment of an industrial
museum. In 1975 the Black Country Living Museum was started by Dudley Borough
Council on 26 acres of totally derelict land adjoining the grounds of Dudley Castle. This
has developed into an award-winning museum which attracts over 250,000 visitors
annually.

It was announced in August 1998 that having secured a lottery grant of nearly £3
million, the Museum Board will be able to authorize the start of work on a £4.5 million
state-of-the-art interpretation centre. This will be known as the 'Rolfe Street Project',
named after the street which once housed the Smethwick Baths. The façade of this
Victorian building is to be incorporated into the new interpretation centre.

At the Black Country Living Museum there is a boat dock fully equipped to restore
narrowboats of wood and iron and different vessels can be seen on the dock throughout
the year. From behind the Bottle and Glass Inn visitors can travel on a canal boat into
Dudley Canal Tunnel, a memorable journey to see spectacular limestone caverns and the
fascinating Castle Mill Basin.

There are 2,500 members of the Black Country Society and all receive the quarterly
magazine *The Blackcountryman*, of which 124 issues have been published since its
founding in 1967. In the whole collection there are some 1,800 authoritative articles on
all aspects of the Black Country by historians, teachers, researchers, students, subject
experts and ordinary folk with an extraordinary story to tell. The whole constitutes a
unique resource about the area and is a mine of information for students and researchers
who frequently refer to it. Many schools and libraries are subscribers. Three thousand
copies of the magazine are printed each quarter. It is non-commercial, and contributors
do not receive payment for their articles.

PO Box 71 · Kingswinford · West Midlands DY6 9YN

CONTENTS

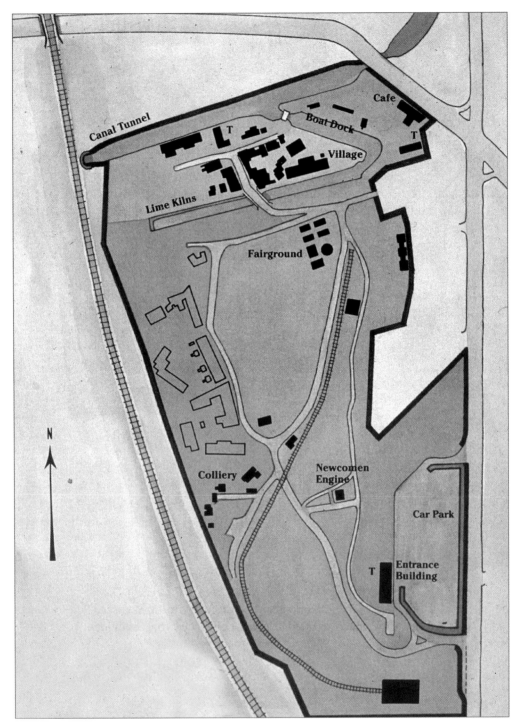

The Black Country Living Museum site.

INTRODUCTION

In the year 2000 the Black Country Living Museum (BCLM) celebrates twenty-five years. The proposal for a Museum was, however, first put forward by the Borough Librarian in Dudley and other interested local individuals in the 1950s. Furthermore, the Black Country Society, founded in 1967 by the late Dr John Fletcher, held a special meeting in 1968 to promote the idea and to bring pressure on the Council. In February 1970, at a public meeting in Dudley Town Hall, the Black Country Society's proposals for the establishing of a Trust Fund and the setting up of a Friends of the Black Country Museum were adopted by the 200 present. Subsequently Dudley Metropolitan Borough Council set up a Black Country Museum section within the Museum Department, which already held some artifacts representing the industrial heritage of the area in the care of the late Richard Traves, who was promoted from Assistant Museums Curator to Keeper of Science and Industrial Archaeology in 1972.

The idea was developed for an open air museum with the aims, as first expressed in its action plan, 'to preserve the past achievements, monuments and products of the Black Country in conjunction with their social background, in order to present a true and permanent record of the region's heritage'. Items could therefore be displayed in their true context as the collections grew. The 26-acre site in Tipton Road was eventually selected and the first portion purchased in 1973, partly because of its proximity to the Dudley Canal Tunnel. In 1975 it was decided to create a Black Country Museum Company separate from the Borough Council, with a sister Development Trust set up to raise funds. The Trust, after careful consideration and advice from Wells of London, decided to raise £600,000 as an initial Founding Fund. Unfortunately this coincided with one of the worst industrial slumps for forty years, but the target was met with 80 per cent coming from only forty-eight donations. The second portion of the site was purchased in the same year, and Ian Walden was appointed as Director of the Museum.

While this type of open air museum seemed novel to England at the time, the first open air museum of buildings in the world had been established at Skansen, Stockholm, as early as 1891 by a teacher, Arthur Hazelius. Concerned that traditional ways of life throughout Sweden were fast disappearing under the impact of industrialisation, he had been collecting extensively in the 1870s to rescue this vanishing culture. In sympathy with his vision of universal education, Hazelius wanted to intensify the experience of history by presenting complete houses, traditionally furnished and equipped and inhabited by authentically dressed people. Skansen now contains over 150 re-erected buildings of many types from all over Sweden. At the museum, glassblowers, silversmiths, weavers and others practise their crafts in appropriate buildings. At Arnhem in Holland another famous pioneering museum contains a good fifty vernacular buildings on a large site. Again, crafts are practised, including papermaking and clogmaking.

In the United Kingdom a number of folk museums were established between the wars, but the 'new breed' of open air museums really dates from the foundation of St Fagan's near Cardiff in Wales in 1946 and Avoncroft near Bromsgrove in England in 1963. Avoncroft has rescued examples of local and not-so-local architecture and removed them to a park, where they have been re-erected and restored to their original condition. This was followed by the establishment in 1971 of a similar museum at Singleton in West Sussex, the Weald and Downland Open Air Museum. Another aspect of our heritage which has become the subject of open air museums is industrial archaeology, a term coined by Midlands lecturer Michael M. Rix in the 1950s. These museums include Ironbridge Gorge, inaugurated in the late 1960s and now operating on several sites – The Furnace, The Warehouse, Coalport China Works and the Blist's Hill area. Others are Beamish, established in the north-east of England (Ian Walden came from there), Abbeydale near Sheffield and Cromford in Derbyshire.

The BCLM combines many of the best ideas of several of its predecessors. From its first beginnings its growth has mushroomed, so that its 26 acre site contains not only a typical Black Country village with other housing, but many industrial exhibits, often with working demonstrators. These include a replica drift coal mine, a working replica Newcomen pumping engine, chain works, steel rolling mill, anchor forge, glass shop, canal-side boat dock and a number of transport items, including a working tramway and trolleybuses.

Commencing in the 1970s, the BCLM has had considerable local support. Industrial and commercial firms have sponsored various projects and the Friends of the Museum, from the outset, not only raised funds and heightened awareness of the proposed museum through talks and other promotions, but also rolled up their sleeves and dredged the canal, and cleared the site of weeds and rubbish. Latterly the Friends dismantled Pitt's Cott from Bilston, rebuilt it on site and manned it with demonstrator-guides. The most recent major project for the museum has been the rebuilding of the former Rolfe Street Baths building from Smethwick, which will provide two large exhibition halls to house both permanent collections and travelling exhibitions. Explanation and interpretation will employ a wide range of modern media. The cost will be £4,274,000, of which the Heritage Lottery Fund is providing almost £3m. When the building was dismantled the Victoria and Albert Museum also contributed £10,000 towards the cost of the preservation and safe transportation to the museum of the highly decorated terracotta façade. This has now been erected alongside the former entrance building and forms the new 'gateway to the past'.

While the BCLM provides a nostalgic experience for older generations, and is an accurate source for study of the history of the Black Country for serious students at home and abroad, it also hosts many groups of school pupils from nationwide who use it as a source for study within the National Curriculum. The museum has a serious purpose and this is reflected in the care which is taken to rebuild or replicate the exhibits on site, even down to the artificial graining on the chainmaker's cottage door. The processes for removing buildings and siting them at the museum have been shown in a number of cases in this book and should give an interesting extra dimension to visitors' and readers' understanding of the Black Country Living Museum.

CHAPTER ONE

THE SITE

Here the dredger bucket is seen in close-up as it clears the canal, 1973. The 26 acres provided for the museum were a derelict former industrial site, which had been used for mining and latterly as a water treatment works. The canal was full of sediment and weeds. (*BCLM*)

Stage I: the future village area photographed from a Snorkel crane in 1974 shows the 'bund' which crossed the canal before the Broad Street bridge was built. (*B. Poole*)

This view of Stage I from the air, ten years later in 1984, shows the bridge completed and the village emerging. (*B. Poole*)

The former waterworks filter beds settling, 1974. (*B. Poole*)

Filter beds for sewage treatment on the site of the future museum. In the foreground is an incinerator, while the large water tanks were constructed by Braithwaite and Kirk. (*BCLM*)

An early view of the top end of the future museum site. After generations of coalmining and latterly of sewage treatment, it was going to need a great deal of clearing before the museum could emerge. In the distance stands the Dudley Guest Hospital, which had been built to deal with industrial injuries. (*BCLM*)

As the museum site had had over forty coalpits and latterly had been used for sewage treatment, there was need for a lot of reinstatement. The canal was blocked, and here a dredger is at work clearing the worst before the Friends of the Museum began their dig-ins in 1973. (*BCLM*)

Looking down the canal from the limekilns end. In the distance dredging has started. Up on the back stands the shunting engine from Pensnett, the *Winston Churchill*, which was the museum's landmark in the early days. (*BCLM*)

The future village site being prepared. In the background to the left the 'bund' blocks the canal, prior to the Broad Street bridge being rebuilt in 1977. (*BCLM*)

Ian Langford shows how much clearing of reeds and rubbish was necessary before the future boat dock site could be established. (*BCLM*)

This appears to be the discovery and rescuing of a narrowboat in 1971. (*BCLM*)

This unpromising view of Stage III, the upper part of the site, was taken in September 1980, when it was derelict. (*BCLM*)

An early school visit reveals in the background how little there was to see at the museum at first and how dramatically it has developed in twenty-five years. (*BCLM*)

A general view of the village site, *c.* 1977. The bridge is in position and the chapel is being built. (*BCLM*)

A very early picture showing the proposed canal dock with builders' sheds still on site, *c.* 1977. (*BCLM*)

A museum open weekend, 1976. The Broad Street bridge stands on site, awaiting rebuilding. (*M. Allen*)

One of the first open weekends which took place in 1975. This picture was taken from the top of the 1842 limekilns and shows the intended village site marked out with tape, indicating the positions of the intended domestic and industrial buildings. (*D.F. Vodden*)

A few years later, in this view, some buildings have already appeared. The chainmaker's house to the left was opened in May 1979. The Oldbury bakery is up, and the shed from Worcester to house the future rolling mill has also been erected. (*D.F. Vodden*)

One year later, in 1980, Gregory's store is centre foreground. Already signs of a local 'miracle' are there; the rapid development of the museum. (*D.F. Vodden*)

CHAPTER TWO

THE VILLAGE:
SHOPS

H. Emile Doo's chemist's shop in Halesowen Road, Netherton before the shop front was dismantled in 1979 and moved to the museum. (*BCLM*)

Here the chapel is almost finished and H. Emile Doo's is under construction, 1979. (*D.F. Vodden*)

H. Emile Doo's chemist's shop interior as displayed at an exhibition in Dudley Museum, *c.* 1973. It shows not only the counter but also the small drawers with crystal knobs for ingredients, the traditional flasks for coloured water and the scales for weighing infants. (*BCLM*)

An early view of H. Emile Doo's chemist's shop frontage in Halesowen Road, Netherton before it was dismantled and brought to the museum in 1979.

H. Emile Doo's chemist's shop re-erected at the museum. When this picture was taken the village street was developing a feeling of permanence, with paved street, the pavement with iron kerbs, and even resident cats. (*D.F. Vodden*)

A rare early view of Gregory's store in Lawrence Lane, Old Hill. (*BCLM*)

From across the canal, before the sweet shop and baker's were built, there was this clear view of Gregory's store on the left. This began as a pair of houses in 1883 in Lawrence Lane, Old Hill. They were built by Charles Gregory, an ironworker. Mrs Gregory began to run a shop probably in a front room. As trade increased the building was converted to provide a double-fronted shop downstairs with living accommodation upstairs. The business passed to the son of the original owner and remained in the family until 1936. It was scheduled for demolition as part of the Lawrence Lane clearance and was dismantled and re-built at the museum, 1979–80. This picture was taken in June 1984. (*BCLM*)

In Gregory's store the demonstrator-guide in costume is bringing the past to life, and being true to the 'living' aspect of the museum. (*D.F. Vodden*)

This view shows how the hardware shop, fish and chip shop and pawnbroker form a street scene typical of the Black Country villages. (*D.F. Vodden*)

No. 34 Piper's Row, Wolverhampton, from Tower Street before it was dismantled and moved to the museum, showing that it was formerly a newsagent's. (*BCLM*)

A view of 34 Piper's Row ground floor taken on the same occasion as the next picture. (*BCLM*)

A view of the first floor of 34 Piper's Row from Tower Street. It shows that a wooden hoarding for advertisements had been affixed over the original, as shown on page 25.

The corner shop, newly rebuilt at the museum. The original site in Wolverhampton had to be cleared to make way for the new Crown and county courts and the police station. It has been set up as a hardware shop, using many unsold items recovered from several stock rooms. (*D.F. Vodden*)

This view of the first floor of the hardware shop was taken from the upstairs window of the rebuilt H. Emile Doo's chemist's shop, and shows clearly the original Gold Flake tobacco advertisement painted on the wall. (*G.R. Phillips*)

Nos 39 and 40 Lower Lichfield Street, Willenhall, which were used as a model for the fish and chip shop at the museum. (*BCLM*)

The fish shop equipment was acquired from a shop in Old Birchills, which had been run by Mrs May Lambourne and her husband Herbert from 1933 to 1954. (*D.F. Vodden*)

Cottages at Himley, showing the extensive damage caused by a lorry crashing into them. They were dismantled and taken to the museum, where they became the pawnbroker's, the hole serving as the shop window. (*BCLM*)

The pawnbroker's shop represents a tradition which was, and is, all too widespread. The contents and interior fittings have been assembled with the help of John Wiltshire, well known as a retailer in the area. (*D.F. Vodden*)

The baker's shop, 50 Birmingham Street, Oldbury, 1910. (*BCLM*)

The bakery is a replica of the shop shown above and no. 48 Birmingham Street is the model for the sweetshop. The original building dates from the 1840s and the shop fronts were added in the 1880s. When you compare this picture with the one above, it can be seen that the building including the door and window on the left have been reversed at the museum. (*BCLM*)

A view from near Gregory's store across the site, 1983. Through the gap, now closed by the pawnbroker's, the Oldbury bakery and the rolling mill shed can be seen. (*M. Allen*)

The Oldbury bakery being rebuilt at the museum, beginning with the oven. This was unusual in design: the oven was actually in the throat of the chimney, so that it heated up very quickly. (*BCLM*)

The cobbler's shop is based on Mr Laurence Davies' shoe repairer's at 24 High Bristol Street, Wolverhampton, where he set up business just before the Second World War. (*D.F. Vodden*)

The demonstration of the cobbler's skills takes place with the aid of Mr Davies' hand tools, and at a bench in front of the window as he would have had it placed. (*BCLM*)

CHAPTER THREE

THE VILLAGE:
CHAPEL, PUB & SCHOOL

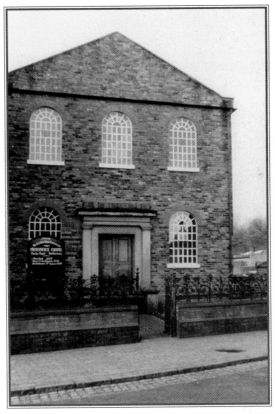

The Darby Hand New Connexion Methodist chapel was one of the first buildings to be rebuilt at the museum. It was originally opened, however, on 29 January 1837. (*D.F. Vodden*)

Providence Church at Darby Hand near Netherton. It belonged to the Methodist New Connexion, very strong in the Dudley area and formed in 1797. (*BCLM*)

The Darby Hand chapel under construction in 1977, just two years after it was closed down. With the aid of photographs, old plans, and using bricks from another chapel, the building was painstakingly rebuilt as accurately as possible. (*BCLM*)

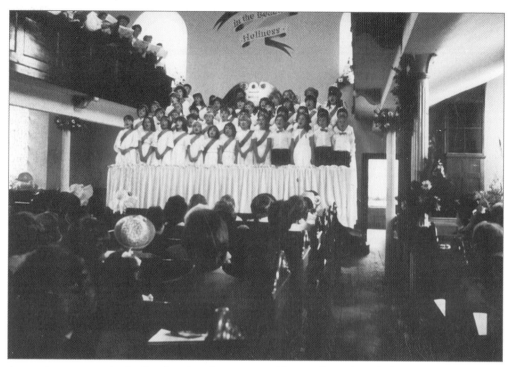

An anniversary service in the chapel at the museum. Harvest festivals and Christmas carol services also now feature in the annual events held at the museum. (*B. Poole*)

A school assembly taking place in the Darby Hand chapel. When booking visits to the museum, schools can request this as a start to the day. (*BCLM*)

The Bottle and Glass on Brierley Hill Road, Brockmoor, by the junction with Moor Lane and Leys Road. It backed on to the Stourbridge Canal at the top of the sixteen locks near Buckpool, and was probably built shortly after the canal was cut in 1776 to 1779. It appears to have been called The Bush in 1822, but was known as the Bottle and Glass by the 1840s and until it closed in 1979. (*BCLM*)

A Snorkel crane being used to dismantle the Bottle and Glass before it was transferred to the museum. (*BCLM*)

The Bottle and Glass under construction, 1981. From then on it has dominated the street. (*M. Allen*)

Canal Street at the museum, 2000. This shows the complete range of shops, with the Bottle and Glass closing the vista. (*D.F. Vodden*)

St James' School, in Salop Street, Eve Hill, Dudley was built in 1842. It ceased to function as a school in 1980 and is shown here being used as a community centre. Because it became structurally unsafe, it closed in 1989. (*BCLM*)

These are the numbered limestone facing stones for the school, illustrating the care taken to dismantle and re-erect buildings accurately. (*D.F. Vodden*)

St James' School from Eve Hill, Dudley under construction, showing how the main building was faced with limestone blocks but the cloakroom's interior wall was of brick, here awaiting plaster. (*D.F. Vodden*)

St James' School from Eve Hill at night, soon after it was rebuilt at the museum – where it was opened in 1992. (*D.F. Vodden*)

HRH the Duke of Gloucester, Patron of the museum, writes on a slate in St James' School during the official opening, 1992. (*BCLM*)

Inside St James' School classroom, modern schoolchildren experience the past. One child was once asked the purpose of the large round inkwell holes on the front of the desk, and answered, 'They are for the computer cables, Miss!' (*BCLM*)

CHAPTER FOUR

THE VILLAGE:
HOUSES

Jerushah Cottage stood at 12 Coopers Bank, Gornalwood. It is named after the last inhabitant, Jerushah Bradley, who died in October 1984. It is tilted because of mining subsidence, which is referred to locally as 'pit-pulled'. (*BCLM*)

This is the south-west front of Jerushah Cottage on 21 April 1986, showing new housing being developed alongside. (*BCLM*)

After Jerushah died the cottage was bought by Cyril and Mary Asprey who, when they couldn't modernise or insure it, gave it to the museum. It took fourteen weeks to dismantle, from March to June 1986. (*BCLM*)

Jerushah being rebuilt. Hundreds of measurements had been taken to ensure that it could be reconstructed accurately. To this end, a cradle was put in position, and frequent checks were made using precise measurements. (*BCLM*)

The front view of Jerushah Cottage being rebuilt. Roof timbers are being fitted, and the cradle is still in place. In the foreground Mrs Mary Edwards looks on. (*J.L. Edwards*)

Jerushah Cottage all prepared for the opening day, which took place on 13 March 1990. HRH the Duke of Gloucester performed the ceremony. (*BCLM*)

Almost as soon as it was opened, Jerushah Cottage proved a leading attraction. Here, some early visitors are filing through in April 1990. (*BCLM*)

Inside Jerushah Cottage, showing the tilt. With an eye for detail, research for a suitable wallpaper pattern culminated at the Walsall Local Studies Centre at Essex Street, as a result of identifying an interior of the period in *Walsall in Old Photographs* by Gilbert and Lewis (Sutton Publishing). (*D.F. Vodden*)

The tilted cottage completely at home in its new location, 28 June 2000. (*D.F. Vodden*)

The two cottages, 97 and 98 Station Road, Old Hill were occupied by two branches of the Newton family. Left to right: George Newton, Florence Newton (née Brookes), Harry Newton, Cousin Ethel, Emma (Granny Newton), Florrie (daughter of Florence), and an American visitor. (*BCLM*)

Replicas of the Station Road cottages, Old Hill, whose building at the museum was funded by Lloyds Bank to mark the bank's first establishment in the Midlands. In the distance is the nailshop dating from about 1880 and brought from Chapel Street, Halesowen. The rebuilding was funded by Marks and Spencer. (*BCLM*)

The Station Road cottages, seen here in 1984, are replicas of the originals which dated from at least 1848. The right-hand unit was occupied by Thomas Newton, a nailmaker. This has been converted to a cobbler's shop by the museum. (*BCLM*)

The rear garden of the Station Road cottages. Volunteers take on the task of maintaining the gardens. The right-hand end cottage has a rear wall partly of limestone, in reality furnace slag. The original builder appears to have built on to a convenient earlier wall. The upper half was of brick, and this has been faithfully reproduced at the museum, in line with their policy of maintaining authenticity. (*D.F. Vodden*)

Pitt's Cott stood at the lower end of Coseley Road, Bilston, close to Alfred Hickman's ironworks. It was probably built by Sam Pitt with his own hands, giving rise to its name. The Pitt family lived here for many years. The cottage was abandoned for a number of years and, becoming ruinous, was rescued in the nick of time by the Friends of the Museum. (From *Bilston, Bradley and Ladymoor in Old Photographs*, Ron Davies and Roy Hawthorne, Sutton Publishing)

Pitt's Cott, re-erected by the Friends of the Museum, was originally built in the mid-nineteenth century. This is also staffed by demonstrator-guides from the Friends. (*D.F. Vodden*)

J.L. Edwards and Lord Dudley, inside Pitt's Cott following the official opening. On the mantelpiece is a spelter ornament, donated by Mr Edwards. Spelter is 50/50 zinc and copper. The figures are inscribed 'La Pavoir' and 'La Force' and date from the late nineteenth century. They originally belonged to Mr Edwards' late mother-in-law, Mrs Lilian Duncan, who lived to the ripe old age of ninety-seven. (*BCLM*)

The Woodsetton tollhouse, 124 Sedgley Road, was built in about 1845 when the Sedgley to Tividale Turnpike was built. (*BCLM*)

The Woodsetton tollhouse at the museum. It has been set in about 1910, when it was the home of a widow, Mrs Nancy Hodgkiss, and her children. (*G.R. Phillips*)

HRH the Duke of Gloucester speaking to Ian Walden in a Brook Street cottage during his visit on 12 May 1992. (*BCLM*)

The iron plates for the cast-iron houses, which were awaiting rebuilding on the museum site. This system of construction was devised after the First World War because it didn't require the traditional skills of building workers, many of whom had been killed during the conflict. (*D.F. Vodden*)

The erection of the cast-iron houses in snow. The rebuilding began with a concrete raft. (*BCLM*)

The cast-iron houses being built in 1991. The exterior had yet to be painted, which had been their original finish, although they were later rough cast. (*BCLM*)

The cast-iron houses were formerly 112 and 114 Birmingham Road, Dudley and were first built in 1925. They were occupied until September 1987 until health inspectors insisted they should be pulled down. (*D.F. Vodden*)

CHAPTER FIVE

INDUSTRY

This is the only full-scale working replica of a Newcomen engine. It was completed in late 1987, and is built within a mile of the first Newcomen engine, which was set up on the Earl of Dudley's mines in 1712. (*BCLM*)

When it was decided to build a replica Newcomen engine there were no examples to copy, so research was carried out using drawings like this. (*BCLM*)

A general view across the top of the site, showing the Newcomen engine under construction. It began to function in March 1986. J.L. (Jim) Edwards, a trustee and formerly of GKN, oversaw the project. (*BCLM*)

To take advantage of modern materials without prejudicing the replica as a whole, R.M. Douglas constructed the interior cross wall as a reinforced concrete slab. This has a notch at the top where the fulcrum for the pump's beam would be placed. On an evening visit by Friends of the Museum, some wag commented, referring to the Douglas stickers, 'He must have been an important man, to have a headstone as big as that!' (D.F. Vodden)

The Newcomen engine operating. Although it doesn't pump water up from the original depth, it is a fine working replica and has won the admiration of the Newcomen Society. (BCLM)

A view of the limekilns, probably photographed in the nineteenth century. Limestone, which was plentiful in the region, was burnt to produce quicklime for use as a fertiliser in agriculture and in mortar for building. (*BCLM*)

The lime kilns were built in 1842 by Lord Ward. To serve them, a special canal arm was dug. There is a lot of limestone locally, including Castle Hill, Dudley, and the sloping wall of the kilns contains typical fossils of the Silurian period. When burnt with the locally available coal, limestone was converted to lime. It is thought that a steam crane was used at one time to load and unload boats and the kilns. Boats were also loaded with crushed limestone for the blast furnaces, roadmaking and for burning elsewhere. This view was originally published entitled 'Black Country Limekilns'. (*BCLM*)

When the trade declined the lime kilns fell into disuse and became overgrown. (*BCLM*)

The lime kilns have now been restored by the museum, with further finance presented by Ian Donald, a Managing Director with GKN, on behalf of the Hayward Foundation. (*J.L. Edwards*)

The rolling mill is housed in a former transport depot building from Worcester, and is designed as a typical Black Country re-rolling mill in which iron, or later steel, bars could be reduced in size or changed in section. The British Steel Corporation donated the mill from its Birchley Works, and the late Keith Gale oversaw the whole project. (*D.F. Vodden*)

The rolling mill in action. This demonstrates very well how it depends on the team of two men working in step with one another, as they pass the glowing rods to and fro through the rollers. (*BCLM*)

This is the scaffolding surrounding the rolling-mill chimney as it was being rebuilt. (*BCLM*)

The demonstration chainshop is not a replica of any original building, but the hearths are copies of two from Noah Bloomer's works in Quarry Bank (using the original ironwork) and one from Cradley Heath. (*BCLM*)

Chainmaking at the restored chainworks, Mushroom Green. This is a satellite site of the museum and demonstrations take place regularly through the summer. At the museum site itself, a set of hearths has been built with better viewing facilities than in an original chainshop. (*D.F. Vodden*)

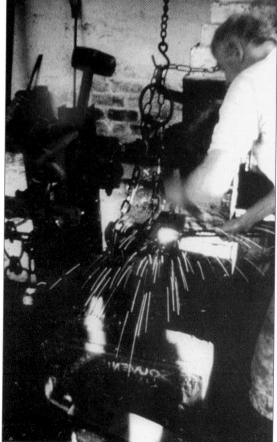

The chainmaker striking on the anvil is producing sparks because the metal is very hot. Making chain by hand is a difficult skill to acquire and at Noah Bloomer's they found that many people cannot develop the knack. (*BCLM*)

These three links are thought to be the test piece for the anchor chain for the *Titanic*, which sank on its maiden voyage in 1912. Here they are exhibited out of doors, but in 2000 they have been transferred to the new exhibition hall. (*D.F. Vodden*)

The *Titanic* anchor being carried on a wagon from Hingley's Netherton works. (*BCLM*)

The original home of Isaiah Preston's anchor forge in Cradley Heath, where it had been installed second-hand in the 1920s. It dated originally from the 1880s. (*BCLM*)

The interior of Isaiah Preston's works, showing the extent of dereliction in the anchor forge with attendant furnace. (*BCLM*)

Isaiah Preston's cranes, which were used for manoeuvring heated iron bars and anchors to and from the hammer. On rebuilding the forge at the museum, new cranes were installed because these wooden ones were unserviceable. (*BCLM*)

Ian Walden helps to operate the anchor forge before its commissioning, which took place on 23 July 1992. (*BCLM*)

The glass-cutter's workshop is a purpose-designed building based on one in Bridge Street, Wordsley. Small glasscutting workshops were found in similar back garden locations in the Stourbridge and Wordsley area, although they wouldn't normally house so many different machines. Glass engraving is a traditional local craft, and is here demonstrated by Paul Bartlett. (*D.F. Vodden*)

HRH the Duke of Gloucester visiting the glass shop during his visit to open St James' School, 12 May 1992. Paul Bartlett is on the extreme right of the picture. (*BCLM*)

A brass foundry from Shaw Street in Walsall. It was originally built in 1869 and was moved to the museum in 1986. (*BCLM*)

The brass foundry roof has an interesting tile pattern, which looks quite attractive. It originates, however, in the need to ventilate the workshop because the process of brass casting sends out very poisonous fumes. Foundrymen used to cough and sweat in bed all night, which was referred to as 'suffering from the sulphur'. (*D.F. Vodden*)

The trap shop under construction. This was formerly Sidebotham's of Wednesfield and was given to the museum in the 1980s when the firm closed down. This was because the use of gin traps was made illegal. The firm had had a considerable export trade and had manufactured traps for catching big cats in Africa – as is shown by destination stencils for their packing cases. (*D.F. Vodden*)

Sidebotham's trap shop interior, showing the hearths and work benches with half-finished traps as they were left when the firm ceased trading. They offered the workshop to the museum in 1982, but it took until 1989 to set it up completely. This was partly because the building had to be shortened to fit the site at the museum. (*D.F. Vodden*)

This building, Lench's oliver shop, was built between 1908 and 1910 and was situated behind a row of houses on the Ross, Blackheath. It was bought in 1937 by T.W. Lench who used six of the ten hearths for making hooks, shackles, clips and fastenings of wrought iron. The workshop was donated to the museum in 1983. (*BCLM*)

Lench's oliver shop has now been rebuilt at the museum with financial aid from the European Regional Development Fund through the Black Country Operational Programme. The first blow by an oliver hammer was struck in July 1993. The oliver is a spring hammer used by blacksmiths and chainmakers. The hammer is connected to a treadle board which is foot-operated, allowing the smith to use it on his own. This device was first referred to in a French document of 1375, but the original meaning of the name is not known. (*D.F. Vodden*)

The Racecourse Colliery is so called because the Earl of Dudley's private racetrack ran across this part of the site before the railway was opened in 1846. It portrays a typical small coal and fireclay mine of about 1900. (*J.L. Edwards*)

The Racecourse Colliery sinking-engine house was used to excavate the old Coneygre 120 coalpit. When it was being painted by a lad using a ladder, he painted between the rungs at one point – hence the white outline of his ladder! (*BCLM*)

Although the museum site covers over forty coal pits, for safety reasons and for the benefit of visitors a replica drift mine has been constructed. Here R.M. Douglas are excavating the site before building a housing for the 'mine' in concrete. The coal mine exhibit is referred to as 'going into the thick' because the principal coal seam locally was 30 ft thick. (*D.F. Vodden*)

The exhibit is populated with waxwork figures with an accompanying taped commentary. This represents a pit boy with Davy lamp and pit pony. (*D.F. Vodden*)

After becoming superfluous at Rubery Owen's Darlaston works in 1970, the lorry chassis press was taken to the Staffordshire County Museum at Shugborough. It is shown here in June 1977 in a field, before being acquired by the BCLM. (*BCLM*)

At the entrance to the museum stands the lorry chassis 1,500-ton press, built by Wilkins and Mitchell and used by Rubery Owen from 1926 to 1970. It was driven by gears and powered by an electric motor. Unusually, it raised steel blanks which were pressed into the chassis shape. (*D.F. Vodden*)

CHAPTER SIX

TRANSPORT

The No. 5 tram by the former entrance building. This single-deck tram ran on the Dudley to Stourbridge system and was built in Tividale in 1920. It was found in a garden in Bennets Hill, Dudley where it had been a summerhouse since coming out of service in 1930. (*D.F. Vodden*)

The *North Star* icebreaker before being moved to the museum. It was salvaged from Ryders Green locks. Detailed records were made of it when it was at the Waterways Yard at Sneyd. (*BCLM*)

North Star was a metal-plated canal icebreaker. It was vital to keep the waterways free during the severe winters because the canals were commercial highways for transporting bulk goods and raw materials. The method of using this icebreaker was to draw it using horses until its bows rested on the edge of the ice. Then, men would board the boat and, using either a rope or chain suspended between the posts, they would literally 'rock the boat' and thus break the ice. The horses would then carry on drawing the boat over the ice so that the process was repeated until the length of waterway was clear. If the ice was more than 4–6 inches thick, everyone waited for a thaw. This picture dates from 1974. (*D.F. Vodden*)

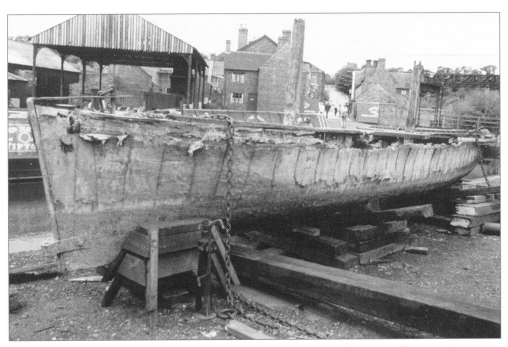

The *North Star* icebreaker under repair. This involved peeling back the metal plating and restoring the timbers underneath. (*D.F. Vodden*)

North Star under repair: the peeling back of the metal plating can be seen clearly here. (*D.F. Vodden*)

Dismantling the lifting bridge in Tipton, 1971. The bridge crossed the railway transhipment basins of Lloyds Proving House near Factory Junction. It was built by Armstrong and Main of Newcastle upon Tyne in 1922. Having been listed as an Ancient Monument, it was first removed to the Staffordshire County Museum at Shugborough and then donated to the museum. The distortion in the uprights in the picture had been caused by vandals swinging the heavy counterweights like pendulums. (*BCLM*)

The lifting bridge in position at the museum before 1985. (*BCLM*)

Peter Keay's boatyard, Walsall, 1975. This was used as one of the models for the museum's boat dock. (*D.F. Vodden*)

A group witnessing the launch of *Birchills* at Malcolm Braine's, June 1977. (*BCLM*)

Narrowboat *Stour* awaiting repair to her timber hull in the boat dock. (*BCLM*)

Here a plank is being softened in the steam chest in the traditional process for building and repairing timber boats. (*BCLM*)

The softened plank is applied to the boat. (*BCLM*)

The plank is finally cramped in position. As it cools, it will retain the necessary curved shape to fit the boat. (*BCLM*)

The stables and tackroom of the carter's yard are under construction, having been donated by Mr and Mrs M.P. Stretton. The project was completed in the next seven days, including installing horses, and was opened officially by James Folkes of Lye on 20 March 1992. (*D.F. Vodden*)

The carter's yard with horse and cart (with rubber tyres) and other stored vehicles, September 1992. Part of the building has now been closed in to form a stable. (*N. Williams*)

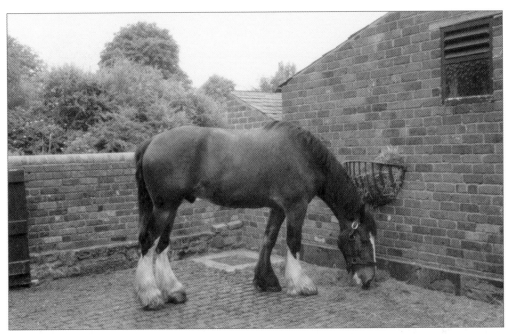

There have been a number of changes of horses at the carter's yard over the years. This is William the carthorse, who was due to pull a canal barge on this afternoon in June 2000. (*D.F. Vodden*)

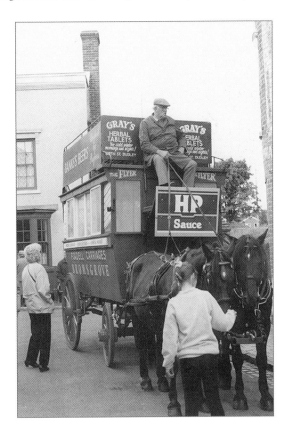

The horse-drawn omnibus, 1994. This is kept at the carter's yard and displays a number of advertisements. HP sauce from Aston takes its name from being 'home produced' – nothing to do with the Houses of Parliament. At the rear there is another notice: 'Unruly children and drunks will be put off!' (*S. Hill*)

Sections of Brown's footbridge on a barge, awaiting erection, 1994. (*BCLM*)

The erection of Brown's bridge in progress, 1994. This bridge was dedicated to the memory of John Clifford Brown, who was an outstanding canal engineer for twenty-five years with British Waterways. He was responsible for many major projects, including the reopening of Dudley Canal Tunnel in 1992. (*BCLM*)

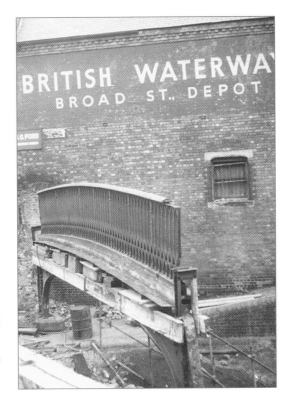

Dismantling Broad Street bridge, Wolverhampton, May 1976. It was first set up in 1879 having been designed by Eastlake Thoms, Borough Engineer, to replace an existing masonry bridge carrying what was then Canal Street over the Birmingham Canal. It was built by Tyldesleys of Willenhall. The main structure was locally produced wrought iron while the outer arches were of cast iron. (*BCLM*)

The erection of the Broad Street bridge from Wolverhampton at the museum. In the picture an outer cast-iron side is in position. (*BCLM*)

A steam roller is used to lay tarmac on the Broad Street bridge. The bridge and its roadway were made narrower when rebuilt. (*BCLM*)

Broad Street bridge today. The narrowboat in the foreground is submerged to preserve its timbers underwater. (*D.F. Vodden*)

The Broad Street bridge is in position in this early picture and the Darby Hand chapel is under construction in the background, dating the scene to about 1978. (*BCLM*)

Len Crane's road roller 'Jane' and a Wolverhampton trolleybus at a museum transport rally. (*N. Williams*)

Tram No. 5 on its first run in 1980, with early museum staff including Dick Hartbury, Stuart Holme, Rob Kendall, John Sherwood, Dave McDougall, Joy Cooksey and Noel Ashley. (*BCLM*)

This tram truck was discovered lying in the grass at Birkenhead and was purchased for the museum. When the transport arrived to collect it, it had already been taken by a scrap metal dealer and the frames severed. The truck was reclaimed, and in the end the severing helped – as it had to be adapted to fit the museum's tram. (*BCLM*)

The Portuguese Oporto tram arrives at the museum
Ian Walden can be seen on top. It was acquired to
provide running gear for the museum trams. (BCLM)

Murphyn Beresford, formerly of Walsall Transport
Department, served as the tram driver early in 1987.
(*BCLM*)

A former tram body is lowered into position to serve as a tram shelter near the Albion depot shed, 1995. (*BCLM*)

A crane lifts a Lisbon tram on its arrival at the museum. This particular tram was to be used for spares. (*BCLM*)

The original Handsworth tram depot
near the Albion ground before removal
to the museum. Only the roof and
upper brickwork were salvaged for the
museum. (*BCLM*)

The tram depot shed in its new location at the museum today. (*D.F. Vodden*)

Inside the Albion tram depot from Handsworth with a museum tram and the museum's Reo bus. (*BCLM*)

Trolleybuses in service at Walsall. Two trolleybuses are regularly run on site: the Wolverhampton 433 of 1946 with a later 1959 body and the Walsall 862 of 1955. (*BCLM*)

These three trolleybuses were part of a 'Trolleybuses Galore' rally at the museum in September 1992. (*BCLM*)

A Car and Bike rally, 7 July 1984. The vehicles were parked on the land of Stage III, where the cast-iron houses and coalmine exhibit are now situated. (*G.R. Phillips*)

Trolleybuses at the original depot, 1984. This building now houses the transport collection and the depot is near the village in the former Albion tram shed. (*G.R. Phillips*)

Sir David Rowe-Ham GBE, President of the Museum Development Trust inaugurating the transport gallery in the former tram depot building, 1995. Museum Chairman Jack Russell is on the left. (*BCLM*)

The 1931 Star Comet, having undergone mechanical restoration by Stan Baggott and Barry Bullock, is here being taken to the Rover Group's Experimental Body Shop at Drewes Lane to have the bodywork restored. The car is now on display in the transport building. (*BCLM*)

The museum's Bean motor car at the May Day Bank Holiday Rally, 1994. Bean built cars in Tipton from 1919 to 1929. (*D.F. Vodden*)

A range of vehicles comprising a tram, trolleybus and a horse and cart on display in June 1992. (*N. Williams*)

HRH the Duke of Gloucester boarding the Bean car with Chairman Desmond Halahan on his first visit, 24 October 1985. On this occasion he opened the museum entrance building. (*BCLM*)

CHAPTER SEVEN

LEISURE

Harts Hill Limelight cinema at 51a Vine Street, Harts Hill, near Brierley Hill, as discovered in January 1982. (*N. Williams*)

Harts Hill Limelight cinema was started in 1921 by John Henry Revill on land adjacent to his house. It was brick-built and cost just under £100. The idea had sprung from his showing films to amuse his children by projecting from outdoors through a window. This shows it in its early days. (*BCLM*)

Harts Hill cinema before dismantling and removal to the museum. (*BCLM*)

Harts Hill cinema before it was dismantled, showing the large entrance porch on the side. The neighbouring building is Rounds' Transport Depot. (*BCLM*)

Ned Williams and Maud Revill, daughter of John Revill who built the cinema, outside the small door which leads into the rewind room and up into the operating box of the Harts Hill Limelight cinema, January 1982. (*N. Williams*)

Harts Hill cinema closed in 1929 and lay forgotten for fifty years. This photograph shows the entrance porch as it is now, rebuilt at the museum at Ned Williams' instigation. (*D.F. Vodden*)

Harts Hill cinema interior, including the simple wooden seats at the front. Tickets for these were originally priced at 2½d and for the tip-up seats at 4d. Now there is free entry for showings of 16mm copies of early films. (*D.F. Vodden*)

The fair has been assembled by David Jones, although his son Dean runs it nowadays for the museum. The fair first opened in 1983, and this is an early funfair layout. (*N. Williams*)

The funfair with a side view of the ark (a high-speed roundabout speedway ride, instead of the traditional animals) and the lighthouse ship, 1 June 1991. (*N. Williams*)

Alan Carter, a member of the Friends of the Museum dressed in appropriate costume, marks out the street for hopscotch, June 1999. (*N. Williams*)

At a Friends' 'live-in' a man helps a child to play a game that involves walking on cans in Canal Street. (*BCLM*)

The Stonefield pigeon loft was Charlie Purslow's pigeon pen, and stood in Prosser Street, Bilston for at least sixty years until its removal to the museum in 1998. The council houses on the right gave way to the new Black Country Route in about 1994. (*R. Davies*)

The Stonefield pigeon loft dates from at least the 1930s. It has been set up near the builder's yard exhibit, which is also from Bilston. (*D.F. Vodden*)

The Rolfe Street Baths, Smethwick is the latest major project to be completed. Incorporating the baths building from Smethwick, it provides two large exhibition halls to house both permanent collections and travelling exhibitions. Explanation and interpretation will employ a wide range of modern media. The cost will be £4,274,000, of which the Heritage Lottery Fund has provided almost £3m. At the time of dismantling this building the Victoria and Albert Museum also contributed £10,000 towards the cost of the preservation and safe transportation to the museum of the highly decorated terracotta façade. (*BCLM*)

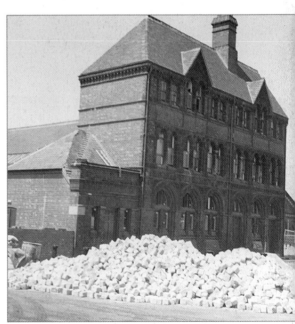

The Rolfe Street building, June 2000.
(*D.F. Vodden*)

The Rolfe Street baths in use. There's many a Blackcountryman who not only learned to swim here but also passed lifesaving tests for medallions. (*BCLM*)

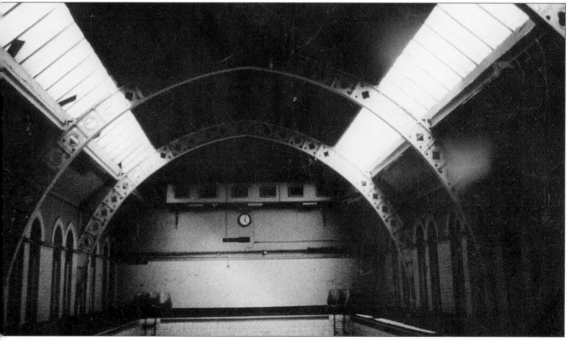

Rolfe Street baths, Smethwick. This was the interior before the removal of the arched roof supports. These have now been incorporated into the new exhibition hall at the Museum. (*BCLM*)

The new entrance to the museum nearing completion, 28 June 2000. (*D.F. Vodden*)

The Rolfe Street complex and the original museum entrance, June 2000. (*D.F. Vodden*)

CHAPTER EIGHT

SPECIAL EVENTS

The topping-out ceremony for the entrance building, February 1984. The façade came from the Hill Top Works, Smith Street, Wednesbury and dated from 1876. Left to right: Ian Walden, Cllr Sparkes, Desmond Hallahan, A.A. Wood (County Architect) and Cllr Hirons. (*M. Allen*)

The steel frame for the new entrance building is erected behind the Hilltop Works façade. This was funded by Dudley MBC and the West Midlands County Council. It was the last Task Force Project at the museum. (*BCLM*)

A view of the museum site with the entrance building on the right. This is now obscured as it has been absorbed into the Rolfe Street project building. The tram used to terminate at the corner of the building, but the track has now been slightly shortened. (*BCLM*)

Keith Bodley makes a speech on behalf of the Transport group on the ten years' anniversary of the running of trams at the museum, 1990. (*BCLM*)

Jack Russell, Museum Chairman, making a speech to Friends and others. In the background is No. 5 Tram, and in the centre of the audience is the late Basil Poole with Margaret Allen, founder members of the Friends. (*BCLM*)

Black Country Society Day, 1994. Stan Hill, Chairman of the Society, explains museum exhibits to Lady Penelope Cobham. (*S. Hill Collection*)

Lady Penelope Cobham with local artist Nigel Hallam at the Black Country Society's Day, 1994. Nigel Hallam, now living in Cornwall, specialises in industrial scenes, but on this occasion he presented a rural landscape as a raffle prize. (*S. Hill Collection*)

Members of City of London livery companies who were making one of their annual visits. Over the years they have made several significant donations towards major projects at the museum. (*S. Hill Collection*)

Two canal boats from the museum near Tower Bridge, 1992 when they were taken to London as part of a promotion of the Black Country Living Museum in the capital. (*I.N. Walden*)

HRH the Duke of Gloucester, Patron of the appeal at the London launch at Natwest Hall, 1990. He had just addressed Masters of the City livery companies. This resulted in funding for such projects as St James' School. (*BCLM*)

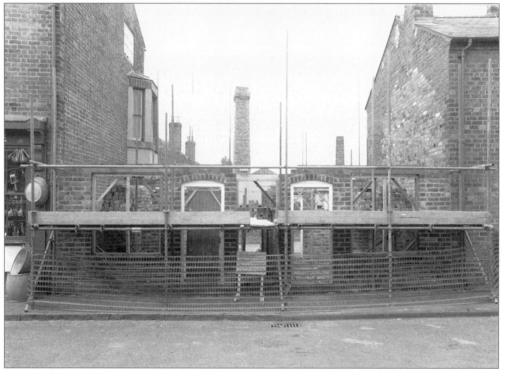

The right-hand side of the village street is at last completed! The fish and chip shop is based on 39 and 40 Lower Lichfield Street, Willenhall (see page 26). Here the replica cottages are being built at the museum. The range came to the museum in 1994 from Old Birchills, Walsall and has been converted to gas from coal-fired to comply with modern hygiene regulations. (*BCLM*)

These views of the village were taken from a snorkel lift at an open weekend. (*J.L. Edwards*)

An early visit by a school party, who are happily reliving the past in their imaginations by wearing period costume. They are being welcomed by the museum guides at the temporary prefab entrance, before the Hilltop building was completed. This took place in 1984. (*BCLM*)

A party of visitors in Victorian/Edwardian costume outside H. Emile Doo's chemist's shop, 1986, looking as though they had been to the chapel on a Sunday. (*BCLM*)

A horse-drawn vehicle alongside the canal at a Boaters' Gathering, 1991. (*BCLM*)

The lifting bridge in operation, being raised to let a narrowboat through at a Boaters' Gathering, 1991. (*BCLM*)

Dudley dig-in by Friends of the Museum with Geoffrey Whittaker, owner of *The Gunner* narrowboat at the top of the picture, 1973. (*BCLM*)

At this very early Steam Weekend the engines certainly made plenty of smoke! (*G.R. Phillips*)

A Steam Weekend, 1983. Vehicles are leaving the village by Broad Street bridge. This was before lamps were added to the bridge. (*G.R. Phillips*)

A steam traction engine, at the same Steam Weekend in 1983 showing the buildings on one side of Canal Street but with the gap, yet to be filled by the sweet shop, baker's, pawnbroker's and fish shop. (*G.R. Phillips*)

Steam traction engine at the May Bank Holiday Steam Weekend, 1994. These annual events are very popular and overflow carparks are brought into use. (*D.F. Vodden*)

Anne Lineen greets HRH the Duke of Gloucester at the opening of St James' School, May 1992. (*BCLM*)

This queue for tea and ices at a kiosk is from the early days of the museum. (*BCLM*)

Ian Walden discussing plans for the new tea room, 1984. This project was to be funded by West Midlands County Council. (*BCLM*)

The Earl of Dudley operating a tipping truck of soil for the turfing over of the coalmine exhibit. (*J.L. Edwards*)

Joe Wiltshire, a prominent local shopkeeper who had given invaluable help in setting up the exhibit, at the pawnbroker's shop opening. (*BCLM*)

CHAPTER NINE

PEOPLE

Lucy Woodhall was the last woman chainmaker. She was born Lucy Swingler in Clyde Street, Old Hill, in November 1899. Her mother was a nailmaker. As a schoolgirl the subject she enjoyed most was needlework and her teacher thought she would do well in dressmaking. She left school at thirteen and started work as an apprentice chainmaker at Hortons in Old Hill. Her wages in the early days for a five and a half day week was 4s. She died in Dudley Guest Hospital in October 1979 aged eighty, having worked until Christmas 1973, which meant she had made chain for sixty years and one month. (*BCLM*)

Lilian Hodgkiss, who was the daughter in the 1910 picture on page 47, sits in front of her former home, the tollhouse. (*BCLM*)

An early picture of a worker carrying out wrought-iron chainmaking. The industry was traditionally located in Dudley and Cradley Heath. (*BCLM*)

J.L. (Jim) Edwards and the rebuilt Anchor Forge. Jim was in charge of this project. It involved him not only in locating such items as a replacement boiler, which came from Walsall Town Hall's heating system, but also in persuading G. Swinnerton, steeplejacks of Stirchley, to rebuild the square chimney-stack to its original height of 66 ft. (*J.L. Edwards collection*)

Friends of the Museum Alan and Jean Carter in the back-to-back cottage. (*BCLM*)

Bessie Hawkes in the kitchen of the chainmaker's cottage, preparing vegetables on the scrubbed kitchen table. (*BCLM*)

Museum staff in costume enjoy the vegetable stall at a market in Canal Street. (*BCLM*)

Jenny Twist carries out a demonstration in the sweet shop, 1991. The drop machine presses different shapes into the wide strip of sugar, so that they can separated into individual novelty sweets. (*BCLM*)

A group of visitors receiving an explanation in the hardware shop. It was on such an occasion that it was alleged by a visitor that after all the children had been bathed in the galvanised bath in front of the fire, 'the whippet went in last'! (*BCLM*)

The baker's shop, with Friends of the Museum acting as counter staff: two lady members and Bert Phillips. (*BCLM*)

Stan Baggott at work as the baker. (*BCLM*)

Brian Wilkes, currently treasurer of the Friends of the Museum, demonstrating the making of nails, 1995. (*BCLM*)

Friends of the Museum, led by Dorothy Pottinger, with a quilt they made and raffled to raise funds in 1978. Left to right: Margaret Allen, Phyllis Bradley, Dorothy Pottinger (designer), Betty Clarke. Others in the team were Anne and Barbara Baggott, Alice Smith, Brenda Poole, Betty Doo, Vera Hickman and her daughter, Elaine Ford. The last two were responsible for putting in the complete lining. (*Express & Star/M. Allen Collection*)

David Owen receives £10,000 for the restoration of narrowboat *Stour* from Mr A.J. de N. Rudge, a Director of Barclays, on 1 February 1991. (*BCLM*)

The Earl of Dudley and the Mayor of Dudley open Pitt's Cott, June 1992. (*BCLM*)

David Owen presents a museum picture to Lord Dudley on his retirement as President. They are watched on the left by Lord Dudley's successor, the Hon. Peter Ward. (*BCLM*)

Desmond Halahan, Chairman of the Museum, Janet Smith and Geoffrey Dean, Chairman of the Friends of the Museum, at the presentation of a narrowboat cabin by the Friends in 1976. (*BCLM*)

W.K.V. (Keith) Gale, Brian Wilkes, Dennis Fellows, Ian Walden and Janet Smith on the delivery of a power hammer at the rolling mill, mid-1980s. (*BCLM*)

From its earliest days the museum has encouraged parties of schoolchildren, and here are two young visitors enjoying the experience in costume. (*J.L. Edwards*)

an Walden makes a presentation to Margaret Allen in the chapel, on 19 April 1986, to mark the twenty-fifth aturday Seminar for teachers run by members of the Education Advisory Panel, of which she was the first hairman. (*Express & Star/M. Allen Collection*)

A school party passing the tram depot on their return from exploring the village in June 2000. (*D.F. Vodden*)

Marilyn McDougall poses in costume in the restored cabin of narrowboat *Diamond*. This boat is kept at the boat dock as a demonstration not only of 'roses and castle' decoration, but also of living quarters for boaters. (*BCLM*)

Adam Baker in costume looking in a shop window in the village, 1982. (*M. Allen Collection*)

Visitors to the museum resting on parts of the Isaiah Preston anchor forge while it was being stored in the rolling mill shed. (*BCLM*)

Don Payne demonstrating hand-wrought chainmaking. (BCLM)

ACKNOWLEDGEMENTS

While the bulk of the pictures for this book celebrating the museum's Silver Jubilee in millennium year come from my lecture slides and the Black Country Living Museum archives, I am indebted to the following for all their help with pictures and information: Freda Allen, Margaret Allen, Alan Cattell, Emma Cook, Ros Corns, Ron Davies, J.L. (Jim) Edwards, *Express & Star*, Vera Hickman, Stan Hill, Stephen Howard, Anne Lineen, Emma Middleton, Bert Phillips, Dorothy Pottinger, Zena Pottinger, R.C. Shayler, Louise Tromans, Ian Walden (who is a mine of information and helped with proofreading) and Ned Williams. Every effort has been made to contact owners of copyright of photographs where it did not rest with those who owned the prints.